Hiram Abiff
King Solomon's Chief Architect & Builder

A Lecture

Keith Moore 32°

Third Degree Tracing Board

ISBN- 978-1-304-84962-5

"Every soul is engaged in a great work-the labor of personal liberation from the state of ignorance. The world is a great prison; its bars are the Unknown. And each is a prisoner until, at last, he earns the right to tear these bars from their moldering sockets, and pass, illuminated and inspired into the darkness, which becomes lighted by that presence"
— Manly P Hall, The Lost Keys of Freemasonry: or The Secret of Hiram Abiff

Hiram Abiff's expertise as a craftsman and his role in the construction of the Temple symbolize the pursuit of knowledge and the honing of one's skills. Maarten Moss

"Know the world in yourself. Never look for yourself in the world, for this would be to project your illusion." ~ Ancient Egyptian Proverbs

"Spirituality Doesn't come from Religion it comes from the Soul." Ancient Egyptian Proverbs

A Replica of King Solomon's Temple

Table of Contents

Introduction

For centuries the architect was the master builder; the one who was responsible for both the design and the construction of a project with sufficient construction expertise to oversee the project from inception to completion. Eventually, the complexity of projects required a higher level of specialization leading to the separation of the designer and the builder. Since that separation, the role of the designer, or architect, has continued to shift and evolve. In recent history, the architect has been the one selected by a building owner, at the inception of the project, as the professional who is able to assist and represent the owner throughout the duration of the project. Today, however, the role of the architect is once again shifting and leading the architect in a different direction. Building owners are beginning to approach the builder through a design-build or construction manager delivery method first and relying upon them for the overall project and construction expertise instead of the architect. The architect will continue to carry the responsibility of creating the building's design and producing the construction documents. It is very unlikely that this role will change. Any of its other construction-related roles, however, are being assumed by the build team. If the architect remains on its current path, it will continue to become more specialized with design and production and carry less responsibility. This lecture focuses on more of an allegory approach. The Masonic degrees attained by the apprentice, fellow craft, and master Mason are increments of knowledge intermingled with science, philosophy, theology, and religion. The symbolism of the First Degree is almost wholly based on the arts and practices of architecture; that of the Second continues to be of the same type, except that in the Middle Chamber Lecture it introduces a set of symbols borrowed from the Liberal Arts and Sciences; in the Third Degree this architectural symbolism retreats into the background to give way to symbolism of another type, one more appropriate to a drama of the soul. Its central symbol is that of a Dying and a Rising Again, a Loss and a Recovery, the theme about which all the Ancient Mysteries were built, and one that stands in this form or that, at the center of all the redemptive religions. In the bare externals of its outward form, it reaches back to the ancient representations of the retreat of the sun in winter, leaving darkness and death behind him and his return in the spring, with healing on his wings, to bestow further light and a new life. However, in its inner essence, it is neither ancient nor modern, but eternal, revealing as it does the way in which the soul recovers from the tragedies of its own failures or misfortunes. The First Degree sets forth the Masonic life as a work of art and teaches the candidate that it is only through a long apprenticeship in obedience to his brothers of a higher elevation that he can learn it—likening him to a youth learning the builder's trade. The Second Degree interprets the Masonic life in the terms of knowledge and wisdom and sets before the candidate the picture of a man in middle life who must possess both knowledge and skill if he is to carry his responsibilities through the heat and burden of the day. Therefore, The Old Testament is very generous to the fellow craft degree. Its primary focus and energy will forever be the building of Solomon's Temple. Though I have extensively covered this subject throughout this project, it would not be of any harm to revisit the second degree of masonry. The Bible from Genesis all the way to the books of ecclesiastics is all the information that gives is foundational Freemasonry. Setting aside the allegory masonry is just pure biblical knowledge intertwines into one cohesive body of knowledge. The Third-Degree cuts to the core of the Masonic life by conducting the candidate through a vicarious experience of tragedy to enable him to discover that the man of evil within a man can be neither trained nor educated out of existence but must die, to the end that the good man in the man shall live. The evil will must perish utterly if ever the good will is to triumph. As a man in old age must lay down his natural life so must the candidate, if ever he is to become a Master Mason in reality, lay down the life of ignorance, of passions, and of the desire to do evil. This is the way of redemption—and the way of redemption is the central theme of the Degree. The Master Mason is the final step of a long journey with both sides of the compass elevated above the square. The final basic degree in which the initiate realizes he himself is a metaphor for Solomon's temple, as well as being shown the Perfect Ashlar, which he is then told represents the opposite of the rough ashlar/cube that he was at the 1st level. He is a perfect ashlar with all the benefits that go with such a privilege. The Master Mason receives all knowledge available to him from his brothers. He is now taught the secrets, which allow him to travel and to utilize the knowledge he acquired over his journey. A true master mason is also an esoteric mason. In this mode he is able to transcend all regular material thinking. He is further blessed with what I call sight beyond sight. Since the master Mason is a skillful person, he has also mastered the use of sacred geometry in his building. This is the real reason why the letter G is place between the square and compass, anything God has ordained it must work to perfection. The first and foremost duty of a Master Mason is to be both a mentor and teacher to those members of a lesser degree. This Master Mason degree is filled with biblical references and its symbols are its teachers. In my opinion, symbols are far superior to written forms of communication because they are visual interpretations, in other words, they are self-explanatory. Masonry is a complete body of work in which the use of signs and symbols are at full display. Symbols have been used for similar purposes and that is to convey some sort of knowledge or meaning only to be understood by a select few. In ancient times this was considered to be more transparent in terms of presenting information to those who were seeking hidden knowledge. The symbols of the craft are definitely ancient in origin. Solomon when was establishing his own institution of masonry he designed it uniquely for the Hebrew hierarchy. This of course was a project which Solomon had inherited from his father David. Throughout the ages, there has always been the establishment of a master and student relationship where one teacher would instruct his student in the knowledge of the chosen craft. This is a constant reminder of how masonry emulates many customs of the ancient world. Our faith in God is what allows us to live in harmony within ourselves and this is the relation between God's sacred geometry. The Bible reminds the Master Mason of the three principal stages of life youth manhood and old age or a grand step to an even greater wisdom. It is reported that King Solomon said that obtaining wisdom is the ultimate accomplishment therefore get wisdom and with all thy understanding. Solomon understood the importance of education and insight. The Bible says he did not pray for wealth or fame but for wisdom and understanding. Wisdom is one of masonry's most important tenets. It being included with strength and beauty tells us that masonry forever reminds us of the qualities that all men should have to exist in this world. Every man regardless of their religion, religious beliefs, and knowledge some force that is far greater than the reality that they know of. Religions centered around a God or gods and these deities are credited with universal powers and account for the operation of universal forces. The Bible forever reminds us of God's universal power. This is self-evident of every event that occurs throughout the ancient biblical world. The Bible was composed of 66 chapters that are divided into two sections the old and the New Testament each testament has within it a series of books divided by historical events. Author Julian Johnson in his book the path of the master's writes the following. "The master is a perfect exemplary for all mankind as to character, nobility, and spirituality. He is the ideal man, and to him all may look for the one perfect example of character and conduct. All may imitate him, follow him implicitly, and then they may rest assured that no mistake will be made. The master is not only a great spiritual light; he is also a perfect man." Johnson continues, "in addition the master is to bring light and love into the world so that all men, not simply his disciples alone but the whole world may profit thereby. "This is part of his secret work, no one may follow him into the secret chamber of his retreat and there see all the features of his great work that he is doing. This spiritual work is for the individual disciples, but he works also for all humankind. The most important relationship the master has is with his Creator. No description of God can ever be given to mortal man. That is because no man can understand such a description if they were given and secondly because no language in the world contains the thought forms necessary. Man on this plane is too limited in comprehension. The reason the master knows so much more about the creator than anyone else is because they have fewer limitations than anyone else. Their capacities and knowledge have been vastly increased during the process of becoming masters. There is not a living being in the entire world who does not receive benefits from a master. A great example of this is Jesus Christ a master to over 5 billion students worldwide. The Bible tells us that it was his usual custom to break away from his disciples to meditate and commune with the Father. It was there he would receive divine instructions on how to carry out his great work. In Masonic allegory, Hiram Abiff did the same thing when he would leave his daily responsibilities and go into his quiet place and draw his designs upon the trestle board for the purpose of building. This sort of thing occurs in every religion. Since then, I have learned that the idea of repurposing is not only done with religious sites but also with religious myths. As such this is a huge example of why Hiram Abiff was included in Masonic symbolism. Author Henry Ridgely Evans In the book Egyptian Mysteries and Modern Masonry writes the following "In Freemasonry, we have the curious legend of Hiram Abiff, the widow's son. The Hiram who cast the great pillars of brass, Jachin and Boaz, which ornamented the portal of Solomon's Temple, and the numerous holy vessels used in the Jewish ceremonial, was not assassinated. Neither in the Bible nor the writings of Josephus is there any account of his dying by violence. The story of Grand Master Hiram Abiff is now regarded as a fable, pure and simple, by all Masonic scholars. It has no historical significance whatever, any more than the story of Isis and Osiris. It is, in the opinion of many eminent authorities, a solar allegory. When, or how, the legend of Hiram came into the Masonic Fraternity is shrouded in mystery. Some claim that it was inherited from the Egyptian Mysteries, through Jewish, Grecian, or Mithraic channels, being a sort of paraphrase of the Osiris myth. It was only natural that as many resemblances between Freemasonry and Mithraism were found, and Mithraism itself was based on astronomical symbolism, so many writers have tried to find astronomy in Masonry. Thus, the twelve fellowcrafts are likened to the twelve signs of the zodiac, and we learn that there was an ancient Egyptian inscription showing a lion seizing a man by the wrist, lying in front of the altar, as if dead. Near the altar stands a man with his left arm elevated in the form of a square.Other writers assert that it was introduced into the craft at a late date, probably during the speculative epoch. The astronomical significance of the legend has been lost to Freemasonry, so far as the explanations of the ritual are concerned. It is a pity! Masonry should not only be in possession of ethical and spiritual truths but scientific as well. Nothing is grander than the contemplation of the heavenly bodies, and facts connected with their mysterious orbits."

The story of Hiram Abiff provides to the Mason a sense of comfort in Masonic Theology. I say this because once a candidate becomes a master mason, he now understands why this Masonic theology exists and why it is used in Masonic ritual. Our ancient ancestors have taught us the same moral lessons we learned in masonry through their mythology. They understood that the information that they left behind was meant to survive through the ages, thereby passing on their knowledge to the next generation. This is an ancient teaching that has manifested throughout the ages and Masonry still follows this manner of teaching. Therefore, this is the most important of all the legends of Freemasonry.

It will therefore be considered with respect to its origin, its history, and its meaning. Before, however, proceeding to the discussion of these important subjects, and the investigation of the truly mythical character of Hiram Abiff, it will be proper to inquire into the meaning of his name or rather the meaning of the epithet that accompanies it.

A Stele of a Phoenician Kin

Chapter I:

King Solomon, King Hiram of Tyre, Hiram Abiff and Phoenician Origins

Our Phoenician ancestors never left anything they undertook unfinished. Consider what they accomplished in their days, and the degree of culture they attained. Ameen Rihani

Located northwest of Nile Valley civilization was the civilization of the ancient Phoenicians. This ancient civilization was well known throughout the ancient world for its ability to sail the seas. As with many other major people groups and empires, the Bible's Phoenicians have their origins in the history of the book of Genesis. The Scriptures have no place as historical data in a certain sense, but they do reveal the symbolic place various peoples had for the narrators at the time of the text's composition.

Phoenicé, or Phoenicia, was the name originally given by the Greeks—and afterwards adopted from them by the Romans—to the coast region of the Mediterranean, where it faces the west between the thirty-second and the thirty-sixth parallels. Here, it would seem, in their early voyaging's, the Pre-Homeric Greeks first came upon a land where the palm-tree was not only indigenous but formed a leading and striking characteristic, everywhere along the low sandy shore lifting its tuft of feathery leaves into the bright blue sky, high above the undergrowth of fig, and pomegranate, and alive. Hence, they called the tract Phoenicia, or "the Land of Palms;" and the people who inhabited it the Phoenicians, or "the Palm-tree people."

The Phoenicians of the Iron Age (first millennium B.C.) descended from the original Canaanites who dwelt in the region during the earlier Bronze Age (3000-1200 H.C.), There is archaeological evidence for a continuous cultural tradition from the Bronze to the Iron Age (1200 -333 s.c.) at the cities of Tyre and Zaraphath. In the Amarna age (fourteenth century B.C.) many letters to Egypt emanated from King Rib-Addi of Byblos, King Abi-Milki of Tyre, and King Zimrida of Sidon, and in other New Kingdom Egyptian texts there are references to the cities of Beirut Sidon, Zaraphath, Ushu, Tyre, and Byblos. Additionally, there is a thirteenth-century B.C. letter from the king of Tyre to Ugarit, and a Ugaritic inscription has turned up at Zaraphath. Despite these facts showing that the coastal cities were occupied without interruption or change in population, the term "Phoenician" is now normally applied to them in the Iron Age (beginning about the twelfth century B.C.) onward when the traits that characterize Phoenician culture evolved: long-distance seafaring, trade and colonization, and distinctive elements of their material culture, language, and script.

The Phoenicians, whose lands correspond to present-day Lebanon and coastal parts of Israel and Syria, probably arrived in the region in about 3000 B.C. They established commercial and religious connections were established with Egypt after about 2613 BC and continued until the end of the Egyptian Old Kingdom and the invasion of Phoenicia by the Amorites (c. 2200 BC).

 Phoenicia also had its greatness for building and astronomy. These Phoenicians (the Canaanites, or Sidonians, of the Bible) were Semitic people. Their country was a narrow strip of the Syrian coast, about 160 miles (260 kilometers) long and 20 miles (32 kilometers) wide. The area now comprises Lebanon and parts of Syria and Israel. Their territory was so small that the Phoenicians were forced to turn to the sea for a living. They became the most skillful shipbuilders and navigators of their time. The Phoenicians began to develop as a seafaring, manufacturing, and trading nation when the Cretans–the first masters of the Mediterranean–were overthrown by the Greeks (*see* Aegean Civilization). Not only did they take the fine wares of the Eastern nations to the Western barbarians, but they also became skilled in making such wares themselves–especially metalwork, glass, and cloth. From a snail, the murex, they obtained a crimson dye called Tyrian purple. This was so costly that only kings and wealthy nobles could afford garments dyed with it. The purple dye was extracted from the secretions of the murex sea snail it was extracted from that creature's glandular mucus. About 10,000 snails were needed to make 1 gram of dye. In ancient times purple dye was 3 times more expensive than gold. It stained the hands of dye workers, earning the name "purple people".

The manufacture of purple dye was a closely guarded Phoenician trade secret, and textiles dyed with it belonged to the most sought-after luxuries among the many precious goods in which the Phoenician merchants traded. They worked the silver mines of Spain, passed through the Strait of Gibraltar, and founded the city of Cadiz on the southern coast of Spain. They sailed to the British Isles for tin and may have ventured around southern Africa. They founded many colonies, the greatest being Carthage. The Ancient city of Carthage was home to the Phoenician mariner. Sailors for the city of

Tyre founded Carthage almost 3000 years ago. However, when we think of Tyre, we can also think of king Hiram of Tyre and Hiram Abiff. They are mentioned in the book of Kings as contributors to God's holy temple. Tyre's name reflects the foundation of its island existence. The basic meaning of the word "Tyre," going back through the Greek and Hebrew words, means "rock."

"According to biblical and Masonic tradition, King Hiram ruled a small but wealthy nation of sea traders to the north of Israel. The cedar beams used in the Temple were cut by woodsmen provided by King Hiram, in the Lebanese forests controlled by Hiram. The King of Tyre also provided trained stone masons who cut and shaped the stone used in the Temple, and the smiths who made the implements, vessels, altar, etc. King Solomon provided unskilled Judean labor, a building site, and wages for the workers.

At the close of the twenty years during which Hiram had assisted Solomon in his buildings, the Israelite monarch deemed it right to make his Tyrian brother some additional compensation beyond the corn, and wine, and oil with which, according to his contract, he had annually supplied him. Accordingly, he voluntarily ceded to him a district of Galilee containing twenty cities, a portion of the old inheritance of Asher, conveniently near to Accho, of which Hiram was probably lord, and not very remote from Tyre. The tract appears to have been that where the modern Kabul now stands, which is a rocky and bare highland, —part of the outlying roots of Lebanon—overlooking the rich plain of Akka or Accho and presenting a striking contrast to its fertility. Hiram, on the completion of the cession, "came out from Tyre to see the cities which Solomon had given him," and was disappointed with the gift. "What cities are these," he said, "which thou hast given me, my brother? And he called them the land of Cabul"—"rubbish" or "offscourings"—to mark his disappointment.

Tyre was a real nation, a Phoenician colony contemporary with biblical Israel. All of this makes King Hiram's crucial supportive role quite odd from the Judeo/Christian viewpoint, as there is no indication that he or any of his people worshipped YHWH. Quite the contrary, like all Phoenician cities, Tyre had its own "Ba'alat" (female goddess) who had a male consort or "Ba'al." Thus, King

Hiram of Tyre, his woodsmen, and his masons were part of the local religious traditions that YHWH's prophets fought against in the Old Testament. "

Author Glen Knape: King Hiram of Tyre

These men were Phoenicians in origin with the exception of Hiram Abiff. He was a man of mixed race and from my understanding; he was part Hebrew and part Phoenician. Understanding the history and the contribution of the Phoenicians will bring us closer to answering how this ancient civilization gave the world so many gifts. I would have to believe that the Phoenicians were a colony of the Ancient

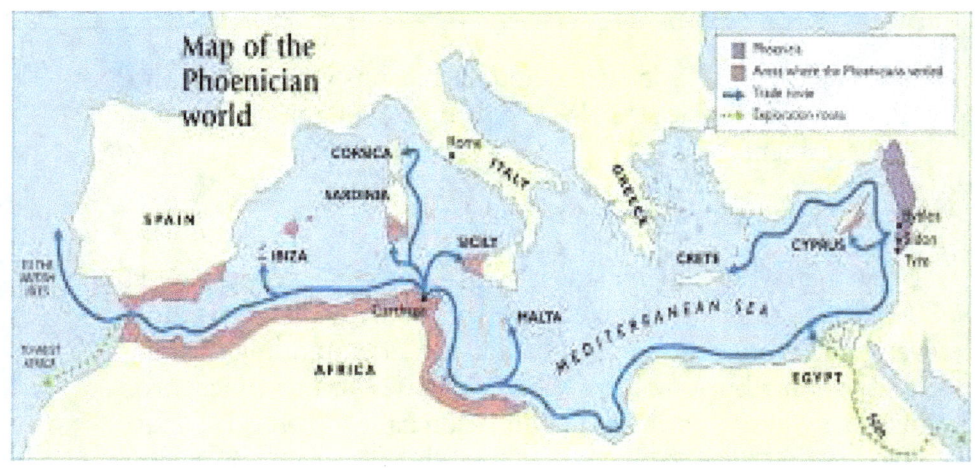

Map of the Phoenician world

Egyptians and just as the Egyptians were Africans so were the Phoenicians and it is possible that the Phoenicians absorbed remnants of Egyptian cultures into their society. "Many Enlighten freemasons may not have known that the Hebrew temple of King Solomon was not built by Hebrews according to the folklore. In fact, it was attributed to none other than Phoenicians. And with the Phoenicians, we get a little closer to the puzzle. The Phoenician builder reputed to be in charge of the building of King Solomon's Temple is Hiram Abiff. Hiram Abiff's attention to sacred geometry, if he was even a real figure, would have come about as a result of Phoenician and not Hebrew deities and beliefs. And here is where we have an interesting link, a number of Phoenician deity's can be traced back to Egypt. Following the expulsion of the Asiatic Hyksos invaders, Egypt becomes for the first time a type of Empire. And she conquers in the direction of the origin of her one-time invaders, towards Western Asia and Phoenicia. There are reports of Egyptian rulers capturing and bringing back Phoenician princes to indoctrinate them in Egyptian beliefs to make vassals of their kingdoms. The Phoenicians become very acquainted with a host of Egyptian gods who either blended in or at times even supplant their own. Pictured here is the Phoenician deity Baal. His demeanor and headdress are specifically Egyptian. Thus, Hiram Abiff's deities and particular ceremonial rituals to sacred geometry and architecture would not have been Hebrew or truly Phoenician, but rather of

The Canaanite God EL - 1,300 B.C.

EL   Baal

Baal was an important Canaanite god, often portrayed as the primary enemy of the Hebrew God Yahweh. The Semitic word "baal" (meaning '"Lord") was also used to refer to various deities of the Levant. Many of the Biblical references designate local deities identified with specific places, about whom little is known. However, in the Bible the term was more frequently associated with a major deity in the Canaanite pantheon, being the son of the chief god El.

Egyptian origin. Once again, Solomon's Temple and Hiram Abiff's existence cannot be proven historically. However, folklore and mythos may tell us a great deal about certain other truths, particularly the linking of sacred geometry with Egypt"

The word temple is derived from the Latin word tempers, time and, therefore, the ancient structures called temples, were, in reality, intended to be records of time and archives of human knowledge. Such institutions would have been a great benefit to ancient societies.

The temple was built of stone quarried and prepared by masons from the Phoenician cities of Tyre and Jbail (Byblos). The stones were cut in the quarry: the Bible tells us not a hammer was heard on the building site as the stones had been shaped so perfectly that they slotted together without being banged into place. The Phoenicians always used huge stones for foundations because the Levant is located on the Great Rift Valley – the big stones helped make buildings earthquake-proof.

The master mason was the architect, too, and had to know geometry. The Master Mason's knowledge was kept secret, known at any given time only to three people. A true master mason is also an esoteric mason. In this mode he is able to transcend all regular material thinking. He is further blessed with what I call the sight beyond sight. One of the major requirements for being a freemason is believing in a supreme being or godhead. Also being steadfast to his belief.

The modern Freemasons' Society developed from the Phoenician masons, which is why their rituals are kept secret. The Freemasons' name the chief mason working on the temple as Hiram Abiff, son of a Tyrian widow, presumably the same person as Hiram the widow's son who did the metalwork. One of the Freemasons' rituals is a re-enactment of the mugging and murder of Hiram in the temple by Israelite workmen who wanted to extract the secrets of architectural design and construction from him. The ritual drama has his assailants attacking Hiram at each corner of the temple with builders' tools before they finally kill him because he won't hand over the secret knowledge.

The Holy Scriptures said that Solomon was a man of wisdom, so in order to have obtained this wisdom, David his father had to have drawn from some of the best educators in the ancient world to teach him.

Before I explore the contributions to Astronomy by the Phoenicians, I must first explore its history in the Masonic order. Phoenician architects brought to Freemasonry the three classes of workmen and they were classed by level of experience and each workman had his place to labor within God's holy temple. Both Hiram of Tyre and Hiram Abiff were men of Phoenician origin. Yet we as members of the Masonic order acknowledge them as major contributors to the craft and its system. Author George Wells Parker writes the following on the ancient civilization of the Phoenicians it states.

"It would not do to neglect the Phoenicians. It is fortunate for the civilization that the chosen people fail to rid the coast of Syria of the race of Canaanites who held it because this race became the most dauntless colonist and mariners of the ancient world. They were the first who turned their frail ships to the mercy of unknown seas, and under the Greek name of Phoenicians explored the known world." I must also include that the Greeks received their alphabet from the Phoenicians. By day, Phoenicians sailors

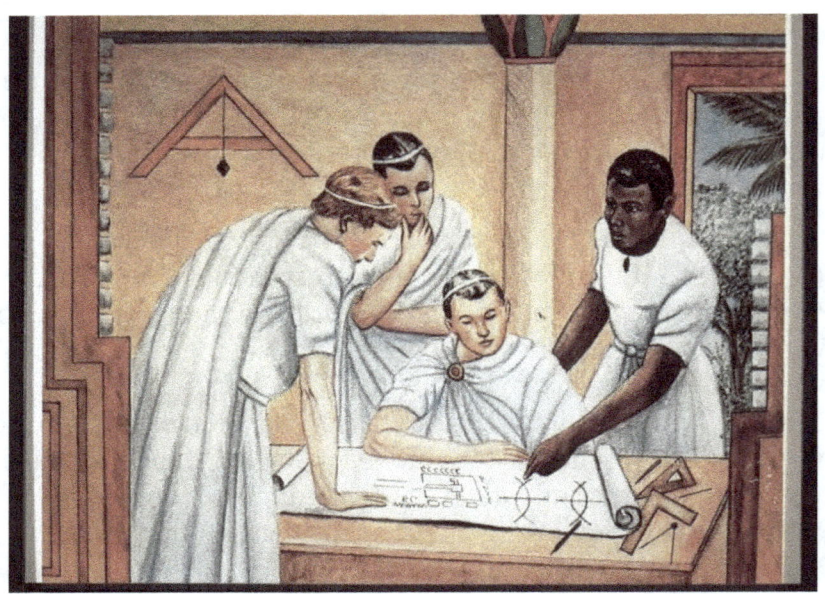

The Phoenician alphabet was composed of 22 letters, with no vowels. The letters were written in a variety of shapes and sizes, including straight lines, curves and circles. This allowed for the creation of different words from the same set of symbols. Phoenician Alphabet is also the origin of Greek Alphabet.

Navigated using landmarks along the coastline. By night they became astronomers using the Phoenicians star also called the North Star in Ursa Minor, the constellation of the little bear. They knew that this star would always be in the Northern sky. This is not intended to be a historical lecture on this race that at first were defined as a mixed race was actually a race of Africans and they were proficient sailors and stargazers. Parker continues:

"It was they, who at a period antecedent to all contemporary historical records, introduced written characters, the foundation of all intellectual development, into that country which was destined to carry intellectual culture to the highest point which humanity has yet reached. It was they who learned to steer their ships by the sure help of the polar star, while the Greeks still depended upon the great bear; it was they who raided the cape of storms and earned the best rights to call it the Cape of Good Hope 2000 years before Vasco De Gama. Their ships returned to their native shores bringing with them trade from the numerous civilizations that they encountered while sailing the high seas. And who are they? Historians might have accepted the legend that their country was settled by Canaanite descendants of Ham and let it go at that. But they were not satisfied to do so. In their desperate effort to take every shred of glory from the African race. They claimed they were Semites. The results of archeology turn their pitiful efforts into something of a joke. Many sarcophagi have been recovered and all reveal the same African features. And the official description of the Sarcophagus or Esmunazar II. King of Sidon and one of Phoenicia's great historical rulers reads, "The features are Egyptian with large full almond shaped eyes. The nose flattened and the lips remarkably thick and somewhat after the Negro mold. The whole countenance is smiling, agreeable and expressive beyond anything I have ever seen in disinterred monuments of Egypt or Nineveh. I leave it to you, gentle reader, if Aryan or Semite ever looked like that."

Along with understanding ancient astronomy among the ancient races what I find difficult is the fact that every civilization that is considered great were either classified as Aryan or Semitic. Yet there is no denying that many of these civilizations were in fact

African in origin. The old terms of Semitic, Hamitic were used to define racial differences both terms were originated from biblical scholars who needed to define the multi diverse people of the bible. From my understanding Semitic means one that is bi-racial, but rather the Phoenicians, Greeks, Babylonians, and Hebrews were a Semitic race. It would be difficult to make this conclusion because there is a presence of African in their blood. George Wells Parker cont., Phoenicia's Greatest Colony was Carthage, "No native orator whose writings have come down to us, has sung of the origin of Carthage, or her romantic voyage; no nature orator has described, in glowing periods. We can still read the splendor of her buildings and the opulence of her nature princess; no native analysts have preserved to the story of her long rivalry with the Greeks and Etruscans and no African philosopher has moralized upon the stability of her institutions or the cause of her fall. Yet, what one of us but has heard the name of Carthage? The love of Dido is forever classic; Hanno's name is secured as one of the worlds earliest and greatest navigators."

The voyages of Hanno King of the Carthaginians illustrate how Phoenicians navigators sailed around the coastlines of Africa discovering settlements on the Western coast of the continent. He may have also reached Europe by way of the North Star as a tool for direction. For his skill in using the stars to explore new worlds, I recognize Hanno as a key representation for all Phoenician mariners, as one of the amazing astronomers of the ancient world. Carthage was also the home of the great African General Hannibal. We cannot think of Carthage unless we think of him. Search all the pages of human history and choose a conqueror who is worthy of a place beside this black general! A man who can create armies out of mercenaries and marches them thousands of miles to the foot of the Alps against the Roman army. So, it would be safe to say that Hanno's story is also one of future legends and he was from the same country as Hannibal. Carthage was located in modern day Tunisia on the African continent. This small seafaring nation was filled notable individuals that we recognize in history. Ancient Phoenicia, a civilization that is visible but invisible in such a way that it has left behind many contributions to ancient history. The bible originally refers to them as Canaanites and these Africans began to expand all across North Africa settling in Libya and other areas in the Atlantic Ocean. The Phoenicians established their capital city Carthage in the Ninth Century. Carthage can be acknowledged as having produced the first real explorer who has written an account of his doings. The adventures of Hanno were said to be equivalent to Homer and his odyssey. Hanno was given command of a fleet of ships to go and establish a chain of colonies on the Atlantic seaboard of Africa. He took sixty ships and thirty thousand men and women who were to settle along the coast. When he came back to Carthage, he wrote an account of the voyage, which was inscribed on a marble tablet and placed in the temple of the city; and this is what he said: "It was decreed by the Carthaginians that Hanno should sail beyond the pillars of Hercules and found cities. Accordingly, he sailed, with sixty ships of fifty oars each, and a multitude of men and women. These are the words of Hanno,

"When we had set sail and passed the pillars after two days voyage, we founded the first city. Below this city lay a great plain sailing thence westward we come to Cape Canton, a promontory of Africa thickly covered with trees. Here we built a temple, and proceeded thence half a day's journey eastward, till we reached a lake, lying not far from the sea, and filled with abundance of great reeds. Here elephants were feeding and a great number of other wild animals. After we had gone a day's sail beyond the lakes, we founded cities, near to the sea. Sailing thence we came to a great river which flows from Africa."

So, from this passage it would seem that ancient Phoenicia had established a working relationship with Africa. The story goes on explaining many relationships between themselves and Africans. So, the Phoenicians were already a great seafaring people when the Israelites finally conquered Canaan and were united under their first king Saul, though they had not reached the full height of their fame till Solomon became King of Israel. Now a great friendship had existed between David, (the poet, writer, King of Israel, and Solomon's father) and Hiram the young king of Phoenicia. And when Hiram heard that King David was going to build himself a palace in is new capital of Jerusalem. Hiram sent him a present of newly filled cedar-trees from Lebanon, together with an offer of carpenters and masons, to help in the building. David accepted both and the skilled workmen from Phoenicia came with their tools to

Jerusalem and worked them. Hiram was a good friend to David, but he was a yet greater friend of Solomon. A treaty of trade was soon established, between the two kingdoms of Israel and Phoenicia. Martin Delaney in his book the Origins and Objects of Ancient Masonry writes the following.

"For the purpose of remedying what is known and conceived to be a great evil in the policy of the world, and for their better government to place wisdom within the acquirement of all men. King Solomon summoned together the united wisdom of the world. He summoned men of all nations and races to consider the great project of reducing the mystic ties to a more practical and systematic principle and stereotyping it with physical science, by rearing the stupendous and magnificent temple at Jerusalem. Previous to the building of the temple, Masonry was only allegorical. It consisted of a scientific system of theories taught through the medium of Egyptian, Ethiopian, Assyrian, and other Oriental hieroglyphics. It was understood only by the priesthood and a chosen few. All the sovereign and members of the royal families were masons, because each member of the royal household had the necessity to be educated in the rituals of the priesthood. And it was not until after masonry was introduced into Asia by the Jews it being strictly forbidden by the Jewish laws for women to be priest that females were prohibited from being Masons."

Phoenicia supplied Israel with wood and craftsmen, and Israel supplied Phoenicia with corn, wine and oil year by year. Phoenicia was growing wealthy, and Hiram set to work and enlarge his capitol Tyre, until it became one of the most beautiful and renowned cities in the ancient world. Tyre and Sidon were already of worldwide fame, when Hiram of Tyre came to the throne of Phoenicia, but much was needed in the way of harbors for the ever-increasing shipping, and to this task, he took upon himself to complete.

Corn, wine, and oil are the Masonic elements of consecration. The adoption of these symbols is supported by the highest antiquity. Corn, wine, and oil were the most important productions of Eastern countries; they constituted the wealth of the people, and were esteemed as the supports of life and the means of refreshment David enumerates them among the greatest blessings that we enjoy, and speaks of them as "wine that maketh glad the heart of man, and oil to make his face to shine, and bread which strengtheneth man's heart" (Psalm civ., 15). In devoting anything to religious purposes, the anointing with oil was considered as a necessary part of the ceremony, a rite which has descended to Christian nations. The tabernacle in the wilderness, and all its holy vessels, were, by God's express command, anointed with oil; Aaron and his two sons were set apart for the priesthood with the same ceremony; and the prophets and kings of Israel were consecrated to their offices by the same rite.

Each of the builders were trained and instructed in all the mysteries of masonry and would therefore competent to teach all the arts of building to the apprentice. And for their wages they were to receive the gift of corn, wine and oil. Let me speak a moment on the wages given to the workers thereof. Corn in ancient times was widely used as a form of compensation. In addition, it was consumed and used to make loaves of bread. References of corn can be seen throughout the Old Testament from the threshing floor of Ornan the Jebusite to the manna and that God gave to the Israelites during their sojourn in the wilderness. One of masonry's most sacred passwords also has a reference to corn and it just so happens that when the word shibboleth was pronounced it was an ancient reference to the word corn. The Bible further speaks of the corn of the heavens, which is the same reference to manna in which the Israelites ate. In Psalms 78:24 verse it speaks about this manna or corn like substance be in the food of the gods it states, "and had rained down manna upon them to eat and had given them the corn of heaven". Psalms 78:25 continues by saying man did eat Angel's food and he sent them me to the full. In Freemasonry, corn is used to consecrate our Lodge Hall because it is one of three things that must be present during the opening of a Masonic Lodge. In Exodus 16:31 manna is described as a flat pancake or wafer. So today this representation of a corn like wafer is used in all forms of religious ceremonies. Manna comes from the tamarisk or palm tree so this tree must produce the ingredients used to make the ceremonial wafers used in communion. This further represents the body of Christ in first Corinthians 10:16 it states:

" The cup of blessings which we bless, is it not the communion of the blood of Christ? The bread which we break, is it not the communion of the body of Christ," so this bread or wafer has an identical reference to a story in ancient Egyptian folklore. The Egyptians called this the Ta heru meaning bread of the Celeste deals or bread of Angels and also Ta en tchet the everlasting bread eaten by the Blessed Which is why it comes from the tamarisk or palm tree. According to Egyptian mythology, Horus was born under a tamarisk or palm tree and this tree was said to have sustained and nursed him until he reached adulthood. Next, we come to the study and full understanding of wine, a beverage that would consume tends to bring forth the hidden emotions of the one who drinks it. It is said that one represents the revelation of God's Spirit filled word. The first miracle Jesus performed was turning water into wine. From that, point on wine is used in all Christian religious practices. Wine represents the blood of Christ and this we can confirm by reading the Last Supper spoken of in the book of Matthew. We know the Jews are well documented in the consuming of wine. The very first reference of one in the Bible came from the story of Noah after leaving the Ark of safety with God's promise to never destroy the world again know was celebrated by indulging in the consuming of wine. Author Corey Gilkes who in his essay the Egyptian great year and Christianity speaks on the story of Noah from an Egyptian kemetic perspective. It states: "Noah's flood is also rich with parallels; the biblical Noah is one who survived the flood, who cultivates wine and becomes drunk. This identifies him with Ausar, sometimes depicted with a bunch of grapes and as an agricultural deity is colored green. The kemetic NU-AKH is the Nile flood that irrigates and cultivates fields. The ark, in one sense, the boats on the Nile, but in its celestial sense, is the barque of the moon that sails across the heavenly flood of the night sky. In its solar mythos, it is the solar boat on its daily course. NUH means drunkenness Ausar was the spirit who possesses the grapes that becomes wine. Wine drinking was reserved for the kemetic priest who, in their intoxicated state would commune with the neter. To this day alcohol is still referred to as a spirit."

Oil like corn and wine is the last piece to this puzzle. Almost all the oil referenced in the Bible refers to olive oil. In ancient times, oil was used for cooking but also for medicine purposes, lighting lamps and religious ceremonies.

When Adam and Eve were in Paradise God sent His Angel to drive them forth. The Angel grieved for them, and when returned to Paradise he thrust the staff into the ground and leaning on it wept bitterly over it. Then the staff grew and in a little while became a tree and the fruit of it was like the tears of the Angel. He ate of it and saw that it was sweet. Then he gave of it to Adam and said to him 'Sow seed of this.' And Adam did so and the name of the tree is the Vine."

The Olive Tree is often called "the Blessed Tree" (El shajarah el mubarakah) and fellahin sometimes swear by it on this wise: "By the Life of the Tree of Light (Whyat shajarah el nur). They believe that the tree is sacred, not sacred as those trees are which are haunted by spirit or 'wely,' but, as the giver of food and light, blessed by God Himself, Who will punish any man who should cut one down so that he should have no peace after. Yet they provoke the Lord daily, not only by cutting wood for fuel, which in His mercy may be pardoned to their need, but by their destroying of beautiful and fruitful trees in the spite of their village feuds. This is the more grievous because the trees take long to grow to maturity for bearing. A man will often in meditating over planting decide to plant figs or other fruit trees rather than olives because he may hope to eat of the fruit of the former himself, while the latter will benefit only his sons. Olives are grown from the shoots round the tree roots and after transplantation and coming to robustness must be grafted. The stocks arc also taken from wild trees and these have a reputation for greater strength, although, of course, the shoots from the cultivated trees are also 'wild' in a sense. This belief in the greater powers of resistance of a wild tree is expressed in the saying, "This one is from a sweet tree" (Hatha min shajara helwe), said of some darling but weakly child as the gossips shake their heads and wonder if it will ever be reared. Oil represents the spirit of Christ in the Bible the oil is the anointing God will bring upon his word. God will anoint them and filled himself with his word. Oil was also used by the prophet Samuel to anoint David King of Israel. Oil from an olive oil tree clearly shows that the olive tree is both revered and yet sacred. Jesus preaches to the masses on the Mount of Olives. The process of removing oil from an olive tree would require skill and perhaps the work of a master tradesman. Olive trees took a long time to grow and mature, but they also lasted for hundreds of years. Therefore, a good oil supply was a sign of stability and prosperity. The lack of oil was a sign of the curse of God and agricultural disaster as a sign of judgment Micah predicted that the nation of Israel "will press olives" but not have the opportunity to "use the oil.

"Touch not mine anointed and do my prophet no harm" as it is written in Psalms 105:15 as quoted from the Bible as proof of how sacred the use of oil is an ancient culture.

In in the eastern world it is still the common use to light churches, mosques and shrines with olive oil in spite of the invasion of modern methods. The lamps are usually of glass, small open vessels, made at Hebron, hung in metal containers, and they are lit by cotton wicks supported by little tin and cark holders soaking in the oil floated on water. Not only is there a blessing on oil vowed and given for this holy use, whether of the 'pure beaten oil' or of whatever quality the donor can afford, but the oil placed in such lamps acquires an added sanctity and is reckoned of curative value. This reminds one of the Story of Marco Polo and how he went to Jerusalem to procure the holy oil from the lamp that hung before the Holy Sepulchre so as to have an acceptable gift for the great Kublai Khan himself. We are not told if he was anointed with the oil or whether he drank it; both uses are known in Palestine and Canaan tells us that at the holy places of "several 'aulia, local saints," the women are not content with merely drinking the oil from the lamps but eat the wicks as well.

These drinking of and anointings with holy oil seem to rise quite naturally from the great esteem in which olive oil is held in daily life. On festive occasions heads are still anointed with oil, and it still drips down the beard and on to the skirts or the clothing; we noted that in the sad recalling of the famine years of the war one of the commonest laments was: "We were so poor we hadn't even a thimble full of oil to put on our heads." Babies, too, are rubbed with oil and salt to make them strong. Did not the Prophet Mohammed himself say "Eat of the oil and anoint yourself with it, for it is from a blessed tree"? So also there are stories and proverbs alluding to the high value of oil, whether used raw or cooked. Old-fashioned people will often begin the day by drinking a little cupful of it, and all are glad to dip their bread in it, and of course to use it in all manner of cooked food. And now a story to show how nourishing olive oil is.

The Holy Bible, a book read by millions, also has a Phoenician connection. In masonry we are constantly seeking light and to further prove this emphasis of the word light the term holy Bible is derived from the Greek word Helios Byblos which means book of sun worship and it is particular meaning out of Africa we are dealing with the worship of amen RA who was represented by the sun and if you've notice in the closing of every prayer, it always ends with amen.

"The Phoenician language seems to have been equally important at that time. A Northwest Semitic language that at one time must have seemed like one of the most important, international, and viable, is today only a faded memory, being preserved almost exclusively in inscriptional material. These languages shared more than linguistic roots and grammatical structure; they shared a poetic and mythological universe. The poetic techniques of their texts, the narrative tropes, and poetic formulae – all of these commonalities point to the existence of a common narrative-mythological poetic stratum to which individual poets or authors from the respective languages and cultures could take recourse."

Ola Wikander Author: Hiram, YHWH, and Baal Freemasonry and the Ancient Northwest Semitic Literary Tradition.

The Phoenician alphabet, like the Hebrew, consisted of twenty-two characters, which had, it is probable, the same names with the Hebrew letters, and were nearly identical in form with the letters used anciently by the entire Hebrew race. This brings us to the question of how both Solomon and Hiram who spoke different languages were able to communicate with each other.

The language of the Phoenicians was very close indeed to the Hebrew, both as regards roots and as regards grammatical forms. The number of known words is small, since not only are the inscriptions few and scanty, but they treat so much of the same matters, and run so nearly in the same form, that, for the most part, the later ones contain nothing new but the proper names.

Earlier I stated that the Greeks borrowed extensively from the Phoenicians for their alphabet. Therefore, Byblos though used, as a Greek word is actually Phoenician in origin.

We must understand the word Helios Byblos and why the word Byblos itself is very important. It is a city that is located in Lebanon that we know was part of ancient Phoenicia. This city is very important for several reasons. One in addition to being called Byblos this is also the location of where the lumber for Solomon's temple came from and in the lore of Freemasonry there could be no Solomon's Temple without the Tall Cedars of Lebanon. Now we must understand that Lebanon was known for its tall Cedars, so the wood was taken from Lebanon was used to make a variety of things but more importantly ancient paper. The Egyptians, the Phoenicians and the Hebrews would travel to this location for the wood to make papyrus or ancient paper. So, think about our modern-day holy Bible, which means Byblos or holy paper. Some of the oldest religious texts written on paper were more than likely prepared from wood taken from this forest. Moreover, to show you how Freemasonry relates to this today we have a Masonic order called the Tall Cedars of Lebanon. Perhaps the most significant contribution of the Phoenicians was a syllabic writing, developed in about 1000 BC at Byblos. From this city's name come the Greek word biblia (books) and the English word Bible. This form of writing was spread by the Phoenicians in their travels and influenced the Aramaic and Greek alphabets. The creation of the Greek alphabet is credit to the Greek hero Cadmus Who was a unique character among Greek heroes.

Cadmus also happened to become the founder of Thebes, after the consultation with the Delphic Oracle who told him to abandon his search for his sister and rather follow his own path. He was also a great warrior and a born leader, not to mention that he was very well educated. Cadmus brought the first alphabetic writing to the Greeks, which consisted of sixteen letters. It was the very first foundation of alphabet in the western world that we know today.

Old Tyre' lay on the seashore, but with rapid growth of trade the sailors of the old town began to use the island which lay close by, and afforded excellent shelter to their ships.

King Hiram had this island enlarged and surrounded by strong walls, which ran out sharply into the sea. He later built harbors one to the north, looking towards Sidon and the other to the South looking towards Egypt, so that in bad weather, when the waves rose high and the winds blew, the merchants of Tyre could reach a safe port.

"The king of Tyre sits like a god in the seat of god," sings Ezekiel, "in the midst of seas. He dwells as in Eden. Precious stones are the covering of his palaces." From a Masonic standpoint, the story further expands the Masonic lore in which the story of Hiram Abiff is at first an allegory tale about the builder of Solomon's Temple. It is a story of trial and error. It instructs the Mason on life, death and rebirth at the same time teaching us to apply this to our moral lifestyle. Allegories are permitted to diverge at will from the facts of history and the teachings of science. Trees may be made to speak, as they do in the most ancient fable extant, and it is no infringement of their character that a worker in brass may be transmuted into a builder in stone to suit a symbolic purpose.

Masonry concentrates on the biblical dealings with God calling both David and Solomon to build his holy temple. This sacred site has numerous significances first; it was the place to which Abraham offered up his son Isaac as a sacrifice to God. Second, it was a future location of God's holy temple. Before construction could begin, David had to find a place where the temple could be erected. First, it was the threshing floor of Ornan the Jebusite that David chose as the future site. He purchased it for 30 shekels of silver. The Jebusites were the people of the threshing floor (a place where grain is threshed). They were a Canaanite tribe who lived in Jerusalem prior to being conquered by David.

The Jebusites were descended from Noah's son Ham, through his son Canaan. They were one of the Amorite tribes who were placed under judgment by God for their wickedness (Genesis 15:16). God described their pagan worship as abominable practices (Deuteronomy 20:18), which may have included child sacrifice. As a result of that judgment, God told the Israelites to exterminate all of the Amorite tribes when they came into the land. The Israelites were also forbidden to intermarry with them, so the Jebusites would not pass on their pagan practices.

The Jebusites dwelt in the hill country, with Jerusalem as one of their key cities (Numbers 13:29; Judges 19:10–11). The Jebusites' name for "Jerusalem" was "Jebus," and it retained that name until the time of King David (1 Chronicles 11:4–5). During the time of Joshua, the Jebusite king Adoni-zedek joined with four other Amorite kings to attack the Israelites at Gibeon (Joshua 10:5), but he was defeated and put to death. Later, the Jebusites joined with Jabin, king of Hazor, in a pitched battle against the Israelites, but they were also defeated by Joshua's army (Joshua 11:3). Despite these defeats, the Jebusites continued to live in the hill country around Jerusalem for many generations. During the time of the judges, some Israelites began to intermarry with the Jebusites, causing God to bring judgment on the nation (Judges 3:5).When David became king of Israel, he attacked the Jebusites of Jerusalem (2 Samuel 5:6) and conquered the city, which then became known as the City of David. Apparently, David granted terms of peace with the remaining Jebusites, because he made a friendly deal with Araunah the Jebusite to purchase land for building the temple (2 Samuel 24:18–25). The Jebusites remained subjugated to Israel and were part of the forced labor Solomon later used for his building projects.

Chronicles 3; 1 states that Solomon began to build the house of the Lord at Jerusalem in Mt Moriah where the Lord appeared unto David his Father. In the place that David had prepared the threshing floor of Ornan the Jebusite. In the Bible uses of the threshing floor, it clearly has two connotations. First, it is a place of blessing. It was the place where the grain of the harvest was actually taken from the sheaves. As such, it was a place where the blessing was received. The Bible refers to "the increase of the threshing floor" (Numbers 18:30) and to a time when "the floors shall be full of wheat" (Joel 2:24). The book of Samuel II will explain David's business dealings with Ornan (Araunah) as well as understand why it was called a threshing floor.A most primitive way of getting the corn out of the ear can be seen occasionally in Trans Jordan and among the tented folk on the coast lands near Caesarea. There the women beat the corn by hand with a wooden mallet, as seen in Plate

3. But in the far distant past some peasant, weary of this tedious labor, had the brilliant idea of making his cattle do the beating for him by the treading of their feet on the bare ground, and this method persists all over the country to this day, for threshing machines are still rare in Palestine.

With harvest time the threshing floor becomes the chief center of village activity, as the empty space, so hard and beaten down, receives the gathered grain. At first the heaps piled on it are small, beans, vetches and lentils are the early ripeners, but hard upon them the real harvest comes in, and the heaps of wheat and barley rise higher and higher till the special place of each family on the floor is full. Then bands of laughing girls climb up on the wheat stack in haste to pull some of the best straws out of the pile before the threshing begins; later, they will sit under shady trees and weave their patterned trays and baskets.

Many of the preparations were made in this undertaking and David's main purpose for building the temple was to show his love for God and to keep a promise that he would establish god's kingdom in strength. Secondly, I believe he owed a great deal to the high priest for their religious advice and guidance. The story further explores the relationship of Hiram king of Tyre and Hiram Abiff a master builder from Tyre who is of mixed race. Architect and builder.

In I Kings 7:13-14, however, the man is simply called (Hiram), King Solomon sent to Tyre and brought Hiram, whose mother was a widow from the tribe of Naphtali and whose father was from Tyre and a skilled craftsman in bronze. Huram was filled with wisdom, with understanding and with knowledge to do all kinds of bronze work. He came to King Solomon and did all the work assigned to him. Craftsmen have always occupied a place of honor in society, dating back to Ancient Egypt, Greece and Rome. Building symbolizes creation, the raising of an edifice in which to glorify and worship gods and humankind and correlates to the improvement of the body and mind as a temple for the soul. Perhaps no building in all history so exemplifies this idea as King Solomon's Temple in Ancient Israel. Hiram Abiff's role in the construction of the Temple was multifaceted. As a master architect, he designed and oversaw the construction of the Temple, ensuring that it adhered to the highest standards of beauty and functionality.

Additionally, as a skilled artisan, he created the Temple's ornate decorations, including the two bronze pillars named Jachin and Boaz. These pillars, which stood at the entrance of the Temple, have become symbols of strength and stability in Freemasonry.

Josephus Antiquities Book 8, Chapter 3, Section 4 (William Whiston Translation 1737): "4. Now Solomon sent for an artificer out of Tyre, whose name was Hiram; he was by birth of the tribe of Naphtali, on the mother's side, (for she was of that tribe) but his father was Ur, of the stock of the Israelites. This man was skillful in all sorts of work; but his chief skill lay in working in gold, and silver, and brass; by whom were made all the mechanical works about the temple, according to the will of Solomon. Moreover, this Hiram made two (hollow) pillars, whose outsides were of brass, and the thickness of the brass was four fingers' breadth, and the height of the pillars was eighteen cubits and their circumferences twelve cubits; but there was cast with each of their chapiters lily-work that stood upon the pillar, and it was elevated five cubits, round about which there was net-work interwoven with small palms, made of brass, and covered the lily-work. To this also were hung two hundred pomegranates, in two rows. The one of these pillars he set at the entrance of the porch on the right hand and called it Jachin (9) and the other at the left hand, and called it Boaz."

Note 11 from William Whiston's translation 1737 "11) Here Josephus gives us a key to his own language, of right and left hand in the tabernacle and temple; that by the right hand he means what is against our left, when we suppose ourselves going up from the east gate of the courts towards the tabernacle or temple themselves, and so vice versa; whence it follows that the pillar Jachin, on the right hand of the temple was on the south against our left hand; and Boaz on the north against our right hand."

Boaz And Jachin

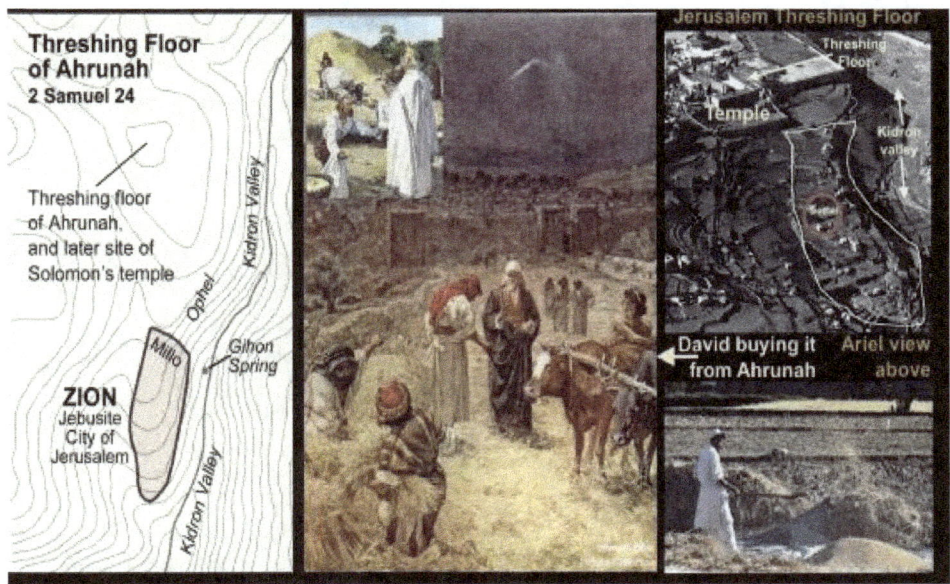

Ornan (Araunah) (Hebrew: אֲרַוְנָה ʾĂrawnā) was a Jebusite mentioned in the Second Book of Samuel, who owned the threshing floor on Mount Moriah which David purchased and used as the site for assembling an altar to God. The First Book of Chronicles, a later text, renders his name as Ornan.

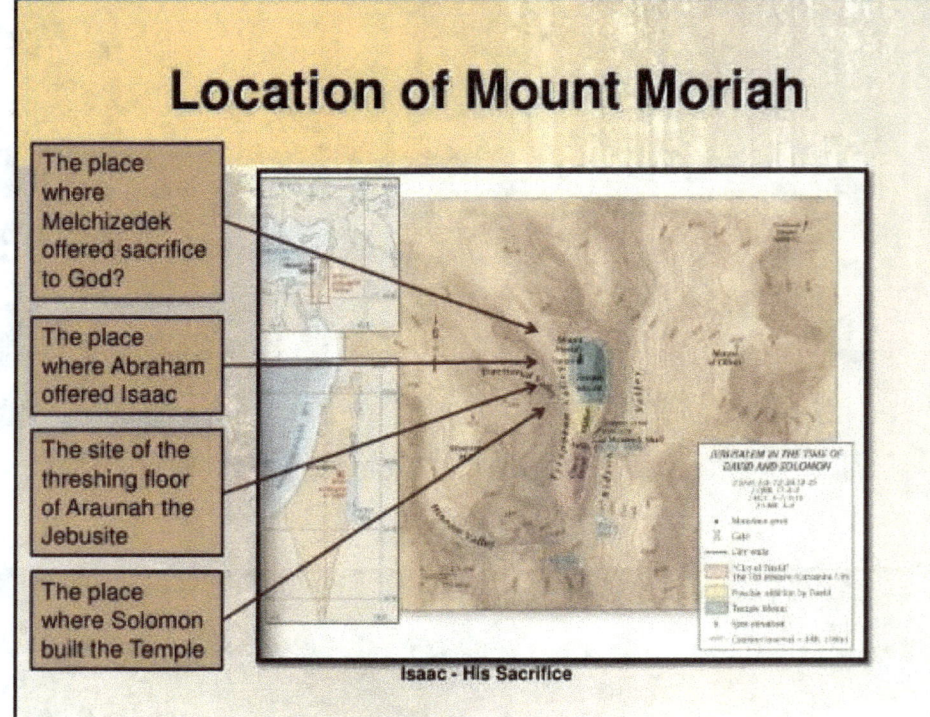

Location of Mount Moriah

The Place where Melchizedek offered sacrifice to God.

The Place where Abraham offered Isaac.

The Site of the Threshing floor of Ornan (Araunah) the Jebusite.

The Place where Solomon built the temple.

The Current site of the Dome of the Rock Mosque in Jerusalem.

Solomon wrote to Hiram of Tyre: Now send me a man with skill in engraving, in working gold, silver, bronze, and iron, and in making blue, purple and red cloth. He will work with the craftsmen of Judah and Jerusalem whom my father David selected. **(2 Chronicles 2:7)** Hiram replied:The son of a woman of the daughters of Dan, and his father was a man of Tyre, skillful to work in gold and in silver, in brass, in iron, in stone, and in timber, in purple, in blue, and in fine linen, and in crimson; also to grave any manner of graving, and to find out every device which shall be put to him, with thy cunning men, and with the cunning men of my lord David, thy father."

A further description of him is given in the seventh chapter of the first book of Kings, in the thirteenth and fourteenth verses, and in these words: I am sending you a wise and skillful master craftsman named Hiram. His mother was a member of the tribe of Dan and his father was a native of Tyre. He knows how to make things out of gold, silver, bronze, iron, stone and wood. He can work with blue, purple, and red cloth, and with linen. He can do all sorts of engraving and can follow any design suggested to him. Let him work with your skilled workers and with those who worked for your father, King David. So now send us the wheat, barley, wine, and olive oil that you promised. **(2 Chronicles 2: 13-15)**

"And King Solomon sent and fetched Hiram out of Tyre. He was a widow's son of the tribe of Naphtali-and his father was a man of Tyre, a worker in brass; and he was filled with wisdom and understanding, and cunning to work all works in brass, and he came to King Solomon and wrought all his work."

The legends of the temple form the cornerstone of Masonry's foundations; but in order to remove any direct references to Judaism or Christianity, the story concentrates on Hiram a man from Tyre who is of mixed races. Hiram was fetched by King Solomon. The book of Kings gives us details. It tells us how the materials for the temple were acquired.

"The cedars of Lebanon were the most famous trees in all of antiquity. They formed the basis of the economy in ancient Lebanon.

Pharaohs from ancient Egypt, kings from Assyria, Babylon and far-flung reaches of the ancient world all clamored for the great timber of these cedars. They were mentioned extensively in connection with the construction of Solomon's First Temple in Jerusalem."

Author Unknown

The lumber was taken from the cedars of Lebanon and escorted down the river Joppa to the temple site.
Afterward, when Operative Art was superseded by the Speculative Science, the latter supplemented to the simple Legend of the Craft the more recondite Legend of the Temple. In this latter Legend, the name of that Hiram whom the King of Tyre had sent with all honor to the King of Israel, to give him aid in the construction of the Temple, is first introduced under his biblical appellation. But this is not the first time that this personage is made known to the fraternity. In the older Legends he is mentioned, always with a different name but always, also, as "King Solomon's Master Mason.
"Author Unknown

In ancient times, cedar wood was especially desirable for its aromatic qualities as well as its resistance to decay and bugs. Lebanon was known for its magnificent cedars and was once heavily forested with them. Cedar was a major export and source of wealth, although, in more recent years, Lebanon has faced deforestation. Even today, the image of a cedar tree is found on the Lebanese national flag.
The cedar wood that was used to prepare the water of separation and to purify leprosy (Leviticus 14:4-7, Leviticus 14:49-52) is illustrative of powerful nations (Ezekiel 31:3, Amos 2:9), the flourishing of saints (Psalm 92:12) and the majesty, strength and glory of Christ (Song of Solomon 5:15, Ezekiel 17:22-23).
Cedar is mentioned throughout the Old Testament as an item of luxury and wealth. David used cedar wood in building his palace (2 Samuel 5:11; 7:2), and it was also used in building the temple (1 Kings 5:6; 2 Kings 19:23), which was almost completely paneled with cedar (1 Kings 6:6, 16, 18, 20, 36). Solomon used it in his Palace of the Forest of Lebanon, with cedar columns, beams, and roof (1 Kings

7:2). It was also used in the construction of the second temple (Ezra 3:7). The abundance of cedar was seen as a sign of prosperity (1 Kings 10:27; 2 Chronicles 1:15.) David and Solomon acquired their cedar from Hiram, king of Tyre, a city in Lebanon (1 Chronicles 14:1; 2 Chronicles 2:3, 8) where the best cedar was to be found.

The fact that God planted the cedars in Lebanon was a sign of His power and goodness (Psalm 29:5; 104:16). His ability to break or burn them is a sign of His power to judge (Zechariah 11:1; Isaiah 2:3; 14:8). Jeremiah warned the king of Judah that, although he rested in a house of cedar—figuratively calling his residence "Lebanon"—he would not escape judgment (Jeremiah 22:14–15, 23).

The cedars of Lebanon were a gift from God and a source of wealth for Lebanon, the cities of Tyre and Sidon especially benefitting from their export (1 Chronicles 17:1, 6; 22:4). Although Tyre and Sidon were on friendly terms with Israel under David and Solomon, in later years they became enemies, and Tyre rejoiced over the fall of Judah. Therefore, God promised judgment (Ezekiel 26).

In the beginning of the 18th century, when what has been called the Revival took place, there was a continuation of the general idea that he was the chief Mason at the Temple; but the true name of Hiram Abif is, as we have already said, then first found in a written or printed record. Anderson speaks of his architectural abilities in exaggerated terms.

He calls him in one place "the most accomplished Mason on earth," and in another "the prince of architects." This character has adhered to him in all subsequent times, and the unwritten Legend of the present day represents him as the, Chief Builder of the Temple," the Operative Grand Master," and the "Skillful Architect" by whose elaborate designs on his trestle-board the Craft were guided in their labors and the edifice was constructed.

Materials came from neighboring countries Egypt, Persia, Nubia etc. But the most important relationship was between Solomon and

Hiram of Tyre. It was through the contributions of the Phoenician King that the workmen and skilled builders were provided to Solomon for his undertaking. Previous to the building of the temple, masonry was only a system of allegory consisting of a system of learning taught through the civilizations of Egypt, Ethiopia, Assyrian, and Greeks. This information was only understood by the priesthood and the elite. Within these civilizations, it seems that members of the Royal family were in a sense mason because each member of the household was required to be educated and initiated in the priesthood. This is why Solomon is so important to Freemasonry. He serves as a prime example of how the ancient orders were established.

in addition, Solomon was a writer of poetry. the numerous chapters in the old testament speaks volumes of his literary contributions.

Take for example the song of Solomon which doesn't have anything to do with freemasonry is an erotic poem, one of the five megillot ('scrolls') in the Ketuvim ('writings'), the last section of the Tanakh. It is unique within the Hebrew Bible: it shows no interest in Law or Covenant or the God of Israel, nor does it teach or explore wisdom like Proverbs or Ecclesiastes (although it does have some affinities to wisdom literature, as the ascription to the 10th century BCE King of Israel Solomon indicates); instead, it celebrates sexual love, giving "the voices of two lovers, praising each other, yearning for each other, proffering invitations to enjoy" The two lovers are in harmony, each desiring the other and rejoicing in sexual intimacy. The women of Jerusalem form a chorus to the lovers, functioning as an audience whose participation in the lovers' erotic encounters facilitates the participation of the reader. Author J.S.M Ward in the book Who was Hiram Abiff writes the following

"Ashtoreth is the same as Astarte , the goddess whose love proved fatal to Adonis , and as late as the time of Ezekiel , c . 594 B.C., we find this prophet denouncing the Jewish women because they wept for Tammuz3 (6) at the North Gate of the Temple. He also denounces the men because within the courts of the Temple itself with their backs towards the Temple of the Lord

and their faces towards the East they worshipped the
sun towards the East. Thus, we can see that the Jews at the time of
King Solomon were far from being strict monotheists, and even the
wise King himself not only did not serve Jehovah with a single eye,
but took care to build shrines for other Gods, perhaps fearing that
otherwise they might be offended . We learn from the Bible itself
that he was actually a worshipper of Astarte , and that , despite
Josiah's herculean efforts later , her worship was not eliminated , for
28 years afterwards the ceremonies connected with the slaying of
Adonis were still taking place .As we shall see later , the " Song of
King Solomon'[1] is undoubtedly a fragment of the ritual connected
with the Rites of Adonis , and the sublime chapter 12 in Ecclesiastes
, which tradition asserts was written by King Solomon , seems to be
connected with the death of Adonis."

Tree of Lebanon

In the Old Testament, the 'true cedar' is mentioned numerous times, adding to the myth and folklore that surrounds this ancient tree. In 1 Kings 4:33, Solomon made the cedar the 'first of trees', while in Isaiah 35:2, the cedar was referred to as the 'glory of Lebanon'. Solomon used the wood of the cedar to build Jerusalem. In 1 Kings 5:6-10, it's said that 'Hiram gave Solomon timber of cedar and timber of fir according to all his desire', while one of Solomon's most important buildings was known as 'the house of the forest of Lebanon' (1 Kings 7:2).

We must remember the Hebrews acquired knowledge from numerous ancient civilizations in order to create their system. Modern day masonry is a celebration of all the ancient orders reminding us that structure is needed in order for any Government to function. At this point the mysteries assumed the name Masonry taken from the building of the temple, and at this time, recognized the universality of the order newly initiated builders could go forth into the world. Then this was the establishment of Masonry, which has been handed down throughout the ages. I can honestly say with no doubt that, many of our biblical stories happened in Ancient Africa or in a region near the mother continent. The origin of Freemasonry can also recognize its African contributions. Just focus on any of the other earlier biblical prophets and their travels of the African continent. Learn of their many interactions with the African people and to prove without a reasonable doubt. Let's reflect on Abraham's travel to Egypt. It was in Egypt where Abraham stayed for a time because famine and starvation had affected his country. (Gen. 12:10-13) He needed a place of refuge because if you knew anything about famine you would know there is a lack of plants (crops) and livestock. So, feeling the heat of starvation, he needed a place to regroup at the same time he had to conceal his identity from the Egyptians by telling his wife to act as his sister. From Abraham to Moses on down to Solomon there were many interactions with African people. The story of Solomon and the Queen of Sheba is yet another example of how ancient scriptures posse the wisdom of old. The story derived from the Bible was early known in Ethiopia, and the Queen of Sheba was venerated as the national ancestress of the Ethiopian people. The story had a long period of gestation and growth there, and the concise biblical account inspired centuries of popular imaginative additions. In addition, the ritual further acknowledges that the ruffians after murdering Hiram tries to escape to Ethiopia by way of a wayfaring man. the Masonic ritual in the Master Mason degree features a drama that is acted out for the candidate, and the role of the Wayfaring Man is one of the shortest ones.

in Masonry, a "wayfaring man" is a Master Mason who has received privileges. The term "wayfaring man" is defined as "one who is accustomed to travel over the roads". It is a phrase that other Master Masons recognize as a solicitation of the Brotherhood.

Ethiopia boasts a 1700 years-old formal educational system. It has a rich written tradition, going back to at least the 300s CE. Ethiopian philosophy and rhetoric witnessed an efflorescence in the 14th century following the ascension into power of the Solomonic Dynasty. Some of the most notable texts to have emerged in this era included the Kebra Nagast (the Glory of the Kings), a volume that unfolds Ethiopian myths of origin, the Tarike Nagast (Royal Chronicles), a text that documents the deeds of Ethiopian kings, the Mashafa Mestira Samay Wamedr (The Book of the Mysteries of Heaven and Earth), a text that sought to explain the creation of the universe, and several anthologies of sermons and hymns.
The 17th century would prove to be another major inflection point in Ethiopian intellectual history. It is in this period that Zera Yacob, reputed by many to be one of Ethiopia's greatest philosophers, wrote his Hatata (Treatise). In this book, Yacob makes a stringent case for a rationalist approach to human inquiry. Yacob, writing in the midst of a relentless campaign of persecution against those opposed to forced religious conversion, argued for a conception of religious faith guided by reason. Walda Heywat, who studied under Yacob, would follow in his teacher's footsteps by writing his own treatise. His book follows his teacher's staunch defense of rationalism and extends his insights into the realm of everyday ethics.
Masonry constantly reminds its members that our foundations come from the Bible and their prophets. Martin Delaney writes the following in his Treatise on Ancient Masonry it states.

"What can be more God like than this, to understand which is to give a man a proper sense of his own importance and consequently his duty to his fellows by which alone, he fulfills the high mission for which he is sent on his temporary pilgrimage? While the Africans, who were the authors of this mysterious and beautiful order, it did much to bring it to perfection by the establishment of the great principles of man's likeness to Jehovah in a triune existence, yet, until the time of King Solomon, there was a great deficiency in his government. In consequences of the policy being monopolized by the priesthood and certain privileged classes or families. For the purpose of remedying what is now conceived to be a great evil in the policy of the world, and for their better government to place wisdom within the acquirement of all men, nations, and races, to consider the great project of reducing the mystic ties to a more practical and systematic principle, and stereotyping it with physical science, by rearing the stupendous and magnificent temple at Jerusalem."

Solomon understood that this ancient system needed to be restructured to the point where it was accessible to all men regardless of their background or origin and who were worthy and deemed qualified. This is an earlier form of Freemasonry. We can truly observe one of masonry's most important principles, that Masonry regards no man for his religion, worldly possessions and wealth.

Let us not forget the establishment of the priesthood in which Solomon confided so heavily in. It was through the blessings of the priest that both David and Solomon were inspired to build the temple in Jerusalem. The bible states that the Levites were the keepers of the priesthood which was originally establish though Jacob's son Levi. Both Moses and Aaron were Levites thus giving us an origin and an establishment of events. Every tribe of Israel has a distinct historical mission. Rather I discuss Joseph's descendant's the Ephramites a tribe whom 4200 of its members were wiped out because of the mispronunciation of a password or Judah's rise to the monarchy of Israel. The Levite had a special role one that there can be on denying it's influenced by an older system of knowledge. No one can ever deny the Kemetic influences throughout the bible, but more importantly how the Levite priesthood was further enhanced while the Hebrew's were in Egypt. We observe the Hebrews in total isolation from the outside world, so there only education was that of Egyptian training. Their borrowing of the Ten Commandments served as a foundation for Jewish law. The first tabernacle in the wilderness could also be of Egyptian design. The bible says that Moses received direct instructions from God on how to design the tabernacle along with being aided by two Hebrews Aholiab and

Bezaleel. In Masonry, they formed what is defined as the holy lodge. Solomon's temple is called the Sacred Lodge. With the education Moses received in Egypt he strengthens the priesthood of the Levites infusing it with new ideas and materials i.e. the Nile Valley civilization. It is self-evident when both Moses and the Egyptian priest turned their perspective staff into snakes. The fact that Moses snake consumed the other snake showed that his powers were stronger, therefore, a stronger God force. I say all of this for a number of reasons. One from an original standpoint and two prior to prior the Hebrews being enslaved there is no written record of them erecting any building structure nor was there any foundation for religious customs until they left the Nile Valley. So, let reflect on the theory of temple building.

This question may be somewhat controversial in understanding Hebrew temple building. We know from biblical scriptures the jews were said to have built the pyramids during their captivity in Israel. One unknown author writes:

"On their way out of Egypt, the Hebrews spent 40 years wandering in the desert of Sinai. During that time all who left Egypt died, including Moses himself who saw the "promised" land but did not live long enough to enter it. Consequently, the Hebrews arrived in Canaan/Phoenicia uncivilized nomads with very little skills or knowledge which civilized people of the area had. By the time they captured Jerusalem c. 1000 BC they have had very little newly acquired capabilities other than fighting wars with the Canaanites/Phoenicians, the Philistines, the Ammonites, the Moabites, the Aramaeans, the Ammonites, the Amalekites and the Edomites."

My question on this subject would be how did they lost the art of building? After leaving the Nile valley? On their way out of Egypt, the Hebrews spent 40 years wandering in the desert of Sinai. During this time all who left Egypt died, including Moses himself who saw the "promised" land but did not live long enough to enter it. Consequently, the Hebrews arrived in Canaan/Phoenicia uncivilized nomads with very little skills or knowledge which civilized people of the area had. By the time they captured Jerusalem c. 1000 BC they have had very little newly acquired capabilities other than fighting wars with the Canaanites/Phoenicians, the Philistines, the

Ammonites, the Moabites, the Aramaeans, the Ammonites, the Amalekites and the Edomites. The Hebrews were not a nation of artisans, but rather of agriculturists, and had, even in the time of David, depended on the aid of the Phoenicians in the construction of the house built for that monarch at the beginning of his reign.

They never had the opportunity to master the art and science of building in Egypt. They were hardened in the desert and in military campaigns but lacked the skill to build palaces worthy of kings or a Temple worthy of God, the Ark of the Covenant, the Tablets of the Law, and the Pentateuch of Moses. These important items of the Hebrew religion were treasured in a tabernacle (tent) up till this point in time.

When David was chosen king and, thereafter, they needed builders and building material, especially wood and precious metals to build a temple and palace. The best known and most gifted people to fulfill the kings' needs were the Phoenicians. Hence, both kings sought and received Phoenician know-how and materials. So, the Hebrew's were once builders and now they depend other civilizations to help them build gods temple. During the height of Egyptian (Kemetic) society one could not enter, instruction of both the Priesthood and the temples until the fundamentals principles of development was understood. This was an important part of the Hebrews experience while in Egypt. I am sure that Moses was not the only Hebrew educated there.

"The Phoenician builder reputed to be in charge of the building of King Solomon's Temple is Hiram Abiff. Hiram Abiff's attention to sacred geometry, if he was even a real figure, would have come about as a result of Phoenician and not Hebrew deities and beliefs. And here is where we have an interesting link, for many a Phoenician deity can be traced back to Egypt. Following the expulsion of the Asiatic Hyksos invaders, Egypt becomes for the first time a type of Empire. And she conquers in the direction of the origin of her one-time invaders, towards Western Asia and Phoenicia. There are reports of Egyptian rulers capturing and bringing back Phoenician princes to indoctrinate them in Egyptian beliefs so as to make vassals of their kingdoms. The Phoenicians become very acquainted with a host of Egyptian gods who either blend in or at times even supplant their own.

Another Phoenicians concept is Hiram Abiff the fabled architect and builder of Solomon's Temple We know, was a widow's son. He was the son of a man of Tyre, but his mother was an Israelite, said in one record to have been of the tribe of Naphtali, and in another, of the "daughters of Dan."

His mother was indeed a native of the tribe of Dan, but her first husband was of the tribe of Naphtali, to whom Hiram was probably born. After the death of the first husband, she then married a man of Tyre, and her son was brought up as a Tyrian and fully educated and trained in the arts of that land. Tyre was one of the principal seats of the Dionysiac fraternity of artificers, a Society engaged exclusively in the construction of edifices and united in a secret organization, subsequently imitated by the Operative Masons of the Temple. Dionysus means "Zeus-limp" and that Hermes named the newborn Dionysus this, "because Zeus while he carried his burden lifted one foot with a limp from the weight of his thigh, and nysos in Syracusan language means limping".

Dionysius is depicted crowned with ivy or vine leaves, riding on a panther or a lion, and bearing in his hand the Thyrsus , the wand entwined with vine branches and surmounted by a fir cone .From this legend we see that Dionysius was originally the Phoenician god of vegetation and the fir cone is particularly characteristic of these Semitic fertility gods . Although we have in this story no account of his death, the fact that he was chased into the sea, and that subsequently he descended into the Underworld and rescued therefrom someone in bondage , clearly shows his true character . His complete identification with the Syrian god is proved, not only by his transformation into a lion, but by the appearance of the bear . As we have already mentioned, Astarte in one of her forms was a Bear Goddess, and in this aspect is depicted at Aphaca about to destroy Adonis. Moreover, the incident of the ship undoubtedly refers to the solar barque , in which the souls of the dead journeyed through the Underworld and on their way often encountered fierce opposition from the powers of evil . Even the incident of his marriage with Ariadne , accompanied as it was by riotous jollifications , brings to mind the ceremonies with which the Great Mother was annually married to her lover. Dionysius was also regarded as patron of the drama and the Dionysian Artificers were named after him . Associated with his name were certain secret rites of initiation connected with his public festival of " The Dionysia .'

Hiram Abiff was quite probably a member of this organization and learned much from this privilege. In assuming his work at Jerusalem, he introduced among the workmen the same exact system of discipline that he had found so advantageous in the Dionysiac Secret Society. From this secret society of operative masons there evolved the Order of Speculative Masons, of which Hiram Abiff was the first Grand Master.

However, what makes the Phoenicians great were their ability to sail the seven seas. They inhabited the coast of North Africa, southern Italy, and parts of Arabia. It was this understanding that we find that the Moors are the descendants of the North African Berbers who in turn were descendants of the ancient Phoenicians as Author George Wells Parker was once quoted as saying "it would not do to neglect the Phoenicians" because it is through this civilization that we learned that the North Africans are descendants of this group of people.

Parker continues "it is fortunate for civilization that the chosen people fail to rid the coast of Syria of the race of Canaanites who held it, because this race became the most dauntless colonists and Mariners of the ancient world. They were the first who turned their frail ships to the mercy of the unknown seas and, under the Greek name the Phoenicians, explored the known world.

In ancient Greek religion and myth, Dionysus is the god of winemaking, orchards and fruit, vegetation, fertility, festivity, insanity, ritual madness, religious ecstasy, and theatre.

Chapter II:

Revisiting the Legend of the Third Degree

"Hiram is presented as the chief architect of King Solomon's Temple, who is murdered in the Temple he was accosted by three ruffians during an unsuccessful attempt to force him to divulge the Master Masons' secret passwords. The themes of the allegory are the importance of fidelity, and the certainty of death." Author unknown

In the structure of Freemasonry, we have the story of Hiram Abiff an allegorical story of a man who was assassinated because he would not reveal the secrets of a higher degree of knowledge to a lesser degree candidate. When we have completed our work, the soul, who has stood near the body, observing its death, is left to decide whether it will return to the body or remain at rest. It, too, is filled with horror at the prospect of the darkness in which it had lived for so long within the body, and this soul knows that it will never again tolerate that former darkness. It can only live in light. The body will pass, but the soul is immortal. The soul now sees itself for what it truly is. It finally agrees to the resurrection. The soul is thus reinterred into the body. This chapter will answer many questions about the Hiram Abiff myth. The founding writers of Masonic literature incorporated Hiram Abiff is an allegorical figure in which it is the portrayal of a pure Masonic tragedy before continuing there are in fact two Hiram's. The first Hiram is mentioned in the book of Kings. This Hiram is where the mason receives the biblical acknowledgment and the historical personification of the Masonic legend. The second or Masonic Hiram Abiff is one that is filled with allegorical teachings that Masons hold true to themselves and to the craft. Hiram, like many other notable men in history of the world, was distinguished in the manner of his allegorical death and what was brought forth was legend, and the dramatic circumstances attending the tragedy are what give amplitude to his biography. Beyond the time, place and means of his murder, Freemasonry knows little about the man, nor apart from Freemasonry when in reality the Biblical Hiram was never murdered but in fact returned to his country after the completion of Solomon's temple and lived a full life thereafter. As masons, we are often questioned on whether Masonry is a religion or is it an esoterically worship of God. People need to first understand exactly what religion is. For the sake of time, I will not cover that definition in this subject matter. What I will say is if you break down the word itself re-means to hold back- ligion means to bind one's will to a set understanding. In some ways, you can call religion a mind control device whose main purpose is to divide the people of world and prevent them from discovering a universal truth. Religion is also a manifestation of an original idea that was eventually added by the practitioners of that religion. As far as the system of Freemasonry the early writers of the order were correct when they made the statement that masonry is not a religion. Albert Pike writes: "Masonry is a worship; but one in which all civilized men can unite; for it does not undertake to explain or dogmatically to settle those great mysteries that are above the feeble comprehension of our human intellect. It trusts in God, and hopes; it believes, like a child, and is humble. It draws no sword to compel others to adopt its belief, or to be happy with its hopes. And it waits with patience to understand the mysteries of nature and nature's God hereafter." Pike says masonry is only a simple worship so when I think of worship a definition can come from a variety of sources. Worship is an act of religious devotion usually directed to a deity it is also an absolute acknowledgement of all that lies beyond us. Therefore, there is something that is more important and far greater than us alone. Now in our society even though we are worshipping a supreme God head for some reason human nature or human error tends to erect objects for us to worship. Sacred shrine buildings and even whole cities are part of this deception. As time continues to move at is pace; sacred sites trend to change religions which is the end result of the controlling party. Allow me to give you an example from an article I was reading. The title of this article is called "Mythology Repurposed."

It states, "Sitting atop of the yet unexcavated part of this temple sits a Catholic church the Iglesia de Nuestra Senora de los Remedios build by Spaniards in 1594. When I asked a professor at the university why the church was built upon a pyramid, I was told that the church simply was built where the people were already coming to worship- that it was an easy way to convert the indigenous population to a new one and unfamiliar religion. I later learned that this is called repurposing a religious site."

This sort of thing occurs in every religion. Since then, I have learned that the idea of repurposing is not only done with religious sites but also with religious myths. As such this is a huge example of why Hiram Abiff was included in Masonic symbolism. Just as the story of Hiram Abiff provide to the Mason a sense of comfort to Masonic Theology. I say this because once a candidate become a master

On the extract before we see the Grand Master sitting on the terrestrial orb with the square in his right hand and the compass in his left, designing a circle on his tracing board, which is a symbol of universality, spanning the whole world with brotherly love. Among other signs, he has drawn the 47th problem of Euclid and a triangle inside a circle. Under his left foot lies a finished plan of a temple. Divine rays are emanating from this figure, as well as from the letter G which is under his feet. G represents both "Geometry" and "God." The Grand Master does not represent Hiram Abiff, but the grand Master Builder himself, the Great Architect of the Universe, designing his eternal plan.

mason, he now understands why this Masonic theology exist and why it is used in Masonic ritual. Our ancient ancestors have taught us the same moral lessons we learned in masonry thru their mythology. They understood that the information that they left behind was meant to survive through the ages, thereby passing on their knowledge to the next generation. This is an ancient teaching that has manifested throughout the ages and Masonry still follows this manner of teaching. In most European Masonic books, I find that the discussion of Freemasonry from its beginning was always defined as primitive masonry which is a term used to define ancient masonry. In reality there is nothing primitive about masonry because modern masonry is built upon the principles of ancient thought. The Hiram Abiff myth becomes in this manner a great story of redemption, which is equivalent to the biblical Prophet Enoch and Elias. Both of whom walked with God and whom God took unto himself, as he takes every soul in this union. You will find that Hiram Abiff will carry on many characteristics. Traditional masonry says that he was a widow's son of the tribe of Naphtali. As a reflection Hiram was of mixed race for, he as part Hebrew and part Phoenician. If you look at the full story of Hiram Abiff and compare it to its biblical version, you will find them to be total opposite. There is nothing else mentioned about Hiram other than once the temple was complete, he returned to his country. But there are others who share the same life and fate of Hiram Abiff. The differences are their stories predate the Hiram myth thousands of years. Now let's finish the allegorical story of Hiram Abiff. Masonic ritual states that he was killed by three ruffians who demanded the secrets of a master mason. Originally there were a total of 15 conspirators who plan to murder Hiram Abiff and out of the 15; three carried out the plan to the end. Next, they take his body and bury it in the rubbish of the temple. Next at low 12 (12 o'clock midnight) they move the body to a hill on top of Hiram was murdered and mutilated. His body was buried on top of Mt. Moriah. The body is situated due east. Due east 6 ft. underground. To identify the location of the body they placed a sprig of acacia on top of the grave. And so we find ourselves at the grave. It has been discovered to contain the body of our lost brother. Planted nearby is a sprig of acacia, which we are told symbolizes immortality. This is a surprising symbol, considering the sight of the body causes the Fellow Craft to turn away in horror.

In the Perfect Elu Degree of the Ancient and Accepted Scottish Rite, Southern Jurisdiction, we learn that
"The acacia...is that genus of trees to which belong that which yields the gum Arabic, the Mesquite, and the locust. It is
the satah or satam wood of the Hebrew writings, used in the construction of the Tabernacle and the Temple4, and therefore a Symbol of Holiness and Divine Truth....It is...not the Symbol of Immortality alone, but of that life of innocence and purity for which the Faithful hope when they shall have been raised up to a new and spiritual existence."

 The men determine that the indecent burial is not sufficient for such an esteemed brother, and so they endeavor to move the body to a proper grave. Their attempts prove difficult since they cannot lift the body without destroying it completely.

Albert Pike, 33° added in the formidable lecture he penned for the Entered Apprentice Degree that the acacia is "the same tree which grew up around the body of Osiris. It was sacred among the Arabs, who made of it the idol Al-Uzza, which Mohammed destroyed. It is abundant as a bush in the Desert of Thur: and of it the "crown of thorns" was composed, which was set on the forehead of Jesus of Nazareth. It is a fit type of immortality on account of its tenacity of life; for it has been known, when planted as a doorpost, to take root again and shoot out budding boughs over the threshold."

Next the Ruffians try to escape to Ethiopia by way of way faring man who turns them away because they did not have permission to leave the country under King Solomon's orders. Then the next 12 fellow craft came before King Solomon informing him that three Ruffians may have carried out the murder of Hiram Abiff and at first, they were originally involved but later recanted. Solomon orders them to search the entire country for the body of Hiram Abiff and next for the Ruffians. The Ruffians were executed, and the body of Hiram was recovered without any signs of the secret world. Next Solomon after two attempts raises Hiram Abiff from the dead with the strong grip of the lion's paw. To resurrect the body of Hiram Abiff, the master's Grip needed to be given.

Finally, after tracking down and executing the killers, King Solomon and King Hiram of Tyre find Hiram's grave, and "raise" his body by use of the Strong Grip of Master Mason or Lion's Paw. Once again, our ritual does not state that Hiram Abiff is brought back to life by

this grip, or that he is admitted to heaven. Instead, we are told that the Kings find and raise his body for the purpose of taking it to the Temple for "more decent interment." Thus, after King Solomon (representative of Wisdom) destroys the illusions of Time (Jubela), Duality (Jubelo) and Space (Jubelum), the Lion's Paw is used to raise the Spirit out of the animated tomb of flesh, and be joined with God by interment in or near his Holy Temple.

It will surprise no one to find that on a dead body, the skin will slip from the flesh, and that the flesh will cleave from the bone. So why did these men attempt to pick up the body? We are told that it was to find more decent interment – but we are never shown that the body was interred afterward. In fact, we are left with the distinct impression that the body no longer requires internment.
Brian Westmoreland in his research paper entitled How to Dispose of a Dead Body- Resurrection and Freemasonry writes the following.

"First comes the requisite dead body, followed by a short-term solution, that of concealing the body. This has immediate benefits, but a permanent solution must be found - an isolated area in which the body will not later be discovered. When the body is discovered, the gig is up, and yet the problem is then transferred to the other party who again faced with the prospect of how to dispose of a dead body. In the end, we aren't explicitly given the answer. And so, we must ask ourselves: How do I dispose of a dead body?

To be sure, there is a final solution to the problem given in our ritual. The search party gathers around the grave, laments the sad state, sends a plea to the heavens, and finally pokes around at the body like an eight-year-old with a stick and a dead raccoon. They discover - to no one's astonishment - that a body left to rot for several days begins to disintegrate - which means it loses its integrity. Horror befalls the searchers, and so they try various means to overcome this process. We witness the story, however, are pulled from the tale and brought back to reality just at the moment in which a solution is proposed. It will surprise no one to find that on a dead body, the skin will slip from the flesh, and that the flesh will cleave from the bone. So why did these men attempt to pick up the body? We are told that it was to find more decent interment - but we are never shown that the body was interred afterward. In fact, we are left with the distinct impression that the body no longer requires internment. The description given is one of Resurrection, or the second rise of the body. Resurrection is a familiar term used in Abrahamic religions, though it is not exclusively used there. Resurrection is commonly misunderstood by those who claim to believe in it.

It is understood that after the murder of Hiram Abiff the master's word was lost. It was lost because each of the Grand Masters (king Solomon, king Hiram of Tyre and Grandmaster Hiram Abiff) had a portion of the word and can only be said when all three are present. Solomon was from the tribe of Judah and their symbol was that of a lion. (Reference Jacob's blessing of his twelve sons). Solomon replaces the lost word with a new secret word. We find ourselves in bodies that are slowly dying. We cannot prevent this deterioration, but we hold hope that we are more than this physical form. As the Greeks taught through the phrase, Soma Sema, the body is a tomb. Our souls are immortal. With that knowledge, we can face our question: How do I dispose of a dead body? The Degree tells us that while three men superintended the building, King Solomon, King Hiram of Tyre, and Hiram Abiff, they possessed in common one secret, and this secret was of such a kind that each man held in his own possession a portion of it necessary to the others. This secret was called a Word, in the ancient sense of the term, not in the

An Egyptian interpretation of Hiram Abiff's Murder

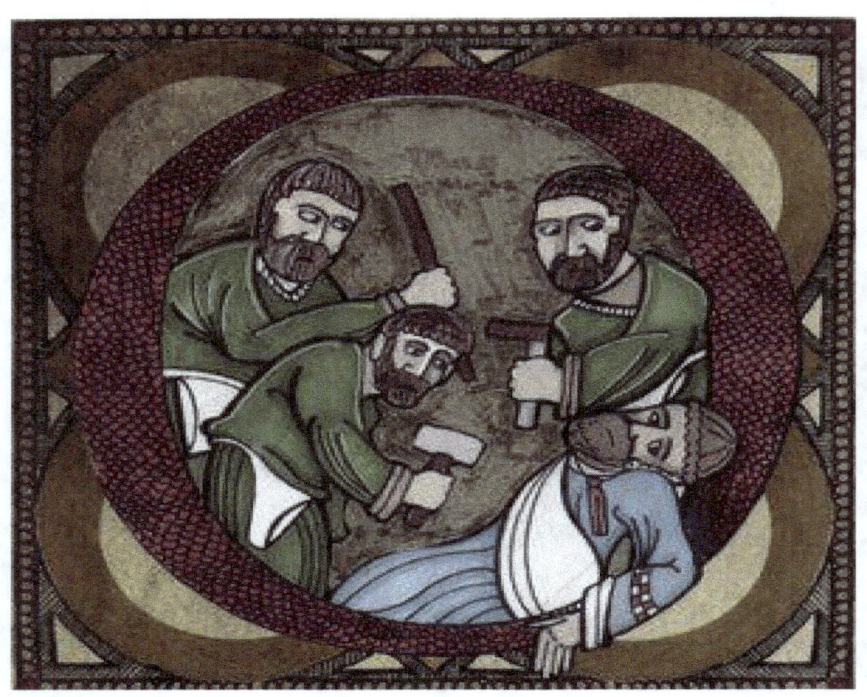

A Medieval Depiction of the Hiram Abiff Drama

A Depiction of the Grand Masters Recovering the body of Hiram Abiff.

modern—that is, it was the knowledge of the power by which such an undertaking could be accomplished. The Tragedy of Hiram Abiff represents the loss of that secret, and the effect of that loss is represented under three aspects: the death of Hiram, confusion among the workmen, and the cessation of work on the building. It was not until a substitute was found that the workmen were brought again into order and the work resumed. Now let's finish the allegorical story of Hiram Abiff. Masonic ritual states that he was killed by three ruffians who demanded the secrets of a master mason. Originally there were a total of 15 conspirators who planned to murder Hiram Abiff and out of the 15; three carried out the plan to the end. Next, they take his body and bury it in the rubbish of the temple. Next at low 12 (12 o'clock midnight) they move the body to a hill on top of Mt. Moriah. The body is situated due east. Due east 6 ft. underground. To identify the location of the body they placed a sprig of acacia on top of the grave. Next the Ruffians try to escape to Ethiopia by way of way faring man who turns them away because they did not have permission to leave the country under King Solomon's orders. Then the next 12 fellow craft came before King Solomon informing him that three Ruffians may have carried out the murder of Hiram Abiff and at first, they were originally involved but later recanted. Solomon orders them to search the entire country for the body of Hiram Abiff and next for the Ruffians. The Ruffians were executed, and the body of Hiram was recovered without any signs of the secret world. Next Solomon after two attempts raises Hiram Abiff from the dead with the strong grip of the lion's paw. To resurrect the body of Hiram Abiff, the master's Grip needed to be given. it is understood that after the murder of Hiram Abiff masters the word was lost. It was lost because each of the Grand Masters (King Solomon, King Hiram of Tyre and Grandmaster Hiram Abiff) had a portion of the word and can only be said when all three are present. Solomon was from the tribe of Judah and their symbol was that of a lion. (Reference Jacob's blessing of his twelve sons). Solomon replaces the lost word with a new secret word.

An important form found among Freemasons is the "Lion's Paw," or grip formed by placing the fingers in the form of a cat's paw. This grip, and its attendant reference to the Lion of the Tribe of Judah, has significance in several respects, both legendary and allegorical.

Its message of transition and everlasting life are a critical part of the Third Degree.

As a symbol, the lion has been a favorite subject prior to the Christian era as well as during the Middle Ages. As a result, there is some confusion regarding its symbolism in Freemasonry. The lion has in all ages been noted as a symbol of strength and sovereignty. The "King of the Beasts," whose mighty roar brought fear to the hearts of all, was known and respected by many ancient cultures. The lion's head and mane were placed on many Egyptian hieroglyphs, idols, and the famous Sphinx, recognizing this animal as the ruler of the animal kingdom. Having the "heart of a lion" was, and is today, deemed an acknowledgment of strength and character. Medieval knights adorned their shields and coats of arms with representations of lions, lion's heads, manes, and paws. Richard, the Lion Hearted, and his famous shield of three lions are well documented, both in history and legend, signifying his sovereignty over England.

As a symbol, the Jews sometimes used the lion as an emblem of the Tribe of Judah as they expected the Messiah to descend from this tribe. This reference carried over to Christianity where the Lion of the Tribe of Judah refers to Jesus Christ, the Messiah. To the ancient craft, this symbolism was seen further in the death and the resurrection to life of man. Legend had that a lion's cub, or whelp, was born dead and brought to life by the roar of its sire. As such, the reference to the lion may be applied to the Messiah, who brought life and the light of immortality to the tribes of Israel, through the roar of God's word.

Albert Pike, in his "Morals and Dogma", gives this interpretation of our legend, saying "The Lion of the House of Judah is the strong grip, never to be broken, with which Christ of the Royal Line of that House, has clasped to Himself the whole human race and embraces them in His wide arms as closely and affectionately as Brethren embrace each other on the five points of fellowship."

Raising the Master,

by Giovanni Battista Barbieri "Il Guercino" (1591-1666).
In possession of the Supreme Grand Chapter of Scotland

THE LION'S PAW IN THE PYRAMID MYSTERIES

The picture shows how the grip of the Lion's Paw was given in the Pyramid Mysteries. The priest wore over his head the mask of a lion. By this grip the spirit in man, long buried in the sepulchre of substance, is raised to life, and the candidate goes forth as a builder entitled to the wages of an initiate.

Picture taken from Manly P Hall's book The Lost Keys of Freemasonry

Resurrection" is a Christian term and a Christian idea. To ask for "resurrection" in ancient Egypt smacks of heresy: of the heresy of reducing the Christian kerygma to just a variant of the Near Eastern myth of dying and rising gods, for example, Osiris whose dying and rising we easily discern the rhythms of nature, such as the sprouting and fading of vegetation, the coming and disappearing of the inundation, the growing and decreasing of the moon, and so on. The description given is one of Resurrection, or the second rise of the body. Resurrection is a familiar term used in Abrahamic religions, though it is not exclusively used there. And in most cases Resurrection is commonly misunderstood by those who claim to believe in it.

The death and resurrection of Christ happened once and for all; it belongs to the course of history and not of nature, to linear not to cyclical time. To be sure, the Egyptian concept of immortality cannot be separated from these natural associations. We are dealing with a religion of divine immanence where natural processes were regarded as divine manifestations. Yet I hope to be able to show that the Egyptian idea of immortality has quite another origin that has more to do with political than with natural theology. In the fame of this new interpretation, the question of possible connections between Egyptian and Christian ideas of resurrection appears in a different light.

The first is of the grand master Hiram Abiff, one of the main builders of Solomon's Temple, which is of spiritual importance. It would be correct to assume that Hiram Abiff observed a spiritual life and full understanding of spirituality, because he was designing and building the Temple that many people will turn to fulfill their spiritual needs. A mason cannot build a perfect hospital if he doesn't have any idea of the needs of the sick! Hiram Abiff's spiritual life made his worldly life different because his joy was in holding firmly to his sets of values bravely even if it resulted in his death.

Surely, Hiram Abiff had the choice to reveal the secrets and escape from his death. Under the circumstances, no one would have blamed him, but for sure, by doing so, he might have lived a miserable and an unhappy life. The Death of the Grand Master Hiram Abiff, is there not to dramatize or to copy sources, or to plant fear in the heart of people. Rather, Death is there to remind us of it. Death is there to remind us of our oath, obligation, and the end of everyone's way.

Bibliography

1. The Holy Bible King James Version Holman's Study Bible

2. The Holy Bible New International Version

3. The Holy Bible Masonic Edition Hertel

4. Baker's Bible Dictionary by Gary Burge and Andrew Hill

5. Baker's Bible Commentary by Tremper Longman III

6. Baker's Bible Handbook by Daniel Hays and J. Scott Duval

7. Children of the Sun by George Wells Parker

8. The Lost Keys of Freemasonry by Manley P Hall

9. Who was Hiram Abiff by J.S.M Ward

10. Resurrection in Ancient Egypt by Jan Assmann

11. King Hiram of Tyre by Glen Knape

12. Hiram Abiff – Man & Myth by Nathan A. Shoff,

13. How to Dispose of a Dead Body- Resurrection and Freemasonry by Brian Westmoreland

14. Egyptian Mysteries and Modern Masonry by Henry Ridgeley Evans

15. The Universal Language of Freemasonry: A Socio-Linguistic Study of an In-Group's Means of Communication compared with Ritualistic Diction and Symbolism of "Profane" Fraternities, and a Survey of its General Applicability by Christina L. Voss

About The Author

Keith L Moore was born in 1973, and raised in the city of Chicago, Illinois. Since 1992, Mr. Moore's primary research interest has been the study of freemasonry and its connection to what he defines as the African Moorish science experience. This exposure gave rise to formation of eastern religions and cultures among blacks in the western hemisphere namely North America. In 1994 he was initiated, passed, and raised to the degree of Master Mason and in 1999 to the 32nd degree of Freemasonry. Mr. Moore has always had a fascination with what he defines as the various studies into the esoteric sides of religions. Mr. Moore is an educator, researcher, and member of several Masonic and afro-centric research societies. Mr. Moore is the author of the following books:

Moorish Circle 7: The Rise of the Islamic Faith among Blacks in America and its Masonic Origins.

Freemasonry Greek Philosophy the Prince Hall Fraternity and the Egyptian (African) World Connection.

Masonic Light from Ancient Africa

Tubal-Cain the Ancient Masonic Blacksmith God

How Egyptian and Moorish Knowledge influenced Western Masonic Thought.

Freemasonry Rosicrucianism & and the Moorish Sufis of the East

About this Book

This work is a historical review of Hiram Abiff and the historical reference to the ancient Phoenicians. Moreover, it examines the dealings between king Solomon King Hiram of Tyre and Hiram Abiff.